10652176

To the Green Man

To the Green Man

POEMS

MARK JARMAN

Sarabande Books
LOUISVILLE, KENTUCKY

Managing Editor
Sarabande Books, Inc.
2234 Dundee Road, Suite 200
Louisville, KY 40205

LIBRARY OF CONGRESS CATALOGING-IN-PUBLICATION DATA

Jarman, Mark.
    To the green man : poems / by Mark Jarman.— 1st ed.
       p.   cm.
    ISBN 1-932511-02-4 (alk. paper) — ISBN 1-932511-03-2 (pbk. : alk. paper)
    I. Title.
    PS3560.A537 T6 2004
    811'.54—dc22
    2003017073

Cover image: *The Wind* by Félix Vallotton, Collection of Mr. and Mrs.
Paul Mellon. Image © 2003 Board of Trustees, National Gallery of Art,
Washington.

Cover and text design by Charles Casey Martin

Manufactured in the United States of America
This book is printed on acid-free paper.

 This project is supported
in part by an award from
NATIONAL
ENDOWMENT
FOR THE ARTS
the National Endowment
for the Arts.

 Partial funding has been provided
by the Kentucky Arts Council, a state
agency in the Commerce Cabinet,
with support from the National Endowment for the Arts.

Sarabande Books is a nonprofit literary organization.

8

FIRST EDITION

811.54
JAR
2004

—M— 8/04 $14—

For my family

CONTENTS

ACKNOWLEDGMENTS

America: Lord Chemistry; *The Atlanta Review:* Psalm 3. *The Atlantic Monthly:* In the Tube, Psalm 5, Canticle, Coyotes; *Blackbird:* Canzone; *Crab Orchard Review:* Goya's *Saint Peter Repentant; Crazy Horse:* Fox Night, The Reckless Father; *DoubleTake:* Dialect; *Five Points:* Over the River and Through the Woods, Visitors; *The Georgia Review:* The Wind; *The Hudson Review:* The Heavenly Ladder of John Klimax, The Excitement, Song of Roland, On Learning of a Child's Memory; *Image:* Psalm 2; *Indiana Review:* In Church with Hart Crane; *The Kenyon Review:* A Pair of Tanagers; *The New Criterion:* Prayer for Our Daughters; *The New Republic:* Astragaloi; *Ploughshares:* To the Green Man, Psalm 1; *Poetry:* Shyness of the Muse in an Almond Orchard, Butterflies Under Persimmon; *Prairie Schooner:* Outside; *Quarterly West:* Psalm 4; *Salt Hill Journal:* George Herbert; *The Sewanee Review:* Kuan Yin, The Secret Ocean; *Slate:* As Close as Breathing; *The Threepenny Review:* Old Acquaintance; *Washington Square:* Testimony of a Roasted Chicken, Summer.

"To the Green Man" is for Philip Wilby. "Dialect" is for Garrett Hongo. "The Excitement" is for Wyatt Prunty. "The Secret Ocean" is for Claire and Zoë. "Summer" is for Amy.

Whisper to me some beautiful secret that you remember from life.

—Donald Justice

To the Green Man

Lord of the returning leaves, of sleepers
Waking in their tunnels among roots,
Of heart and bush and fire-headed stag,
Of all things branching, stirring the blood like sap,
Pray for us in your small commemorations:
The facet of stained glass, the carved face
Lapped by decorations on the column side,
And the entry in the reference book that lists you
As forester, pub sign, keeper of golf courses.
King for a day, or week, then sacrificed,
Drunk on liquor made from honey, urged
To blossom at your leisure, and caressed—
The temptation is to think of you without envy.
In Fewston, Yorkshire, near the open moor,
You are set in a church window above the altar.
Wreathed and strangled, amber-glazed, you wear
A look of non-surprise, a victim's cunning,
Though your tongue hangs as dumb as any death.
Elsewhere, when you make your appearances,
Out of your mouth stems and oak leaves grow—
Like speech or silence? Your eyes are empty cups.
Pray, vestige-secret of the trees, for us,
Surprised and pleased to find you any place.

Testimony of a Roasted Chicken

Standing in drizzle in the twilit piazza,
Beside the lean Franciscan with his P.A. system,
One of the hilltown's aging bachelors,
Rumpled and plump and damp and pompadoured,
Tells the buzzing mike, the falling rain
And darkness, about Jesus, *la via, la verità, la vita.*
From lit-up bars, a few of us look out at him,
Knowing and pitying and finally indifferent.

How different, later in the bakery,
—Saturday night, buying Sunday's bread—
When he, the sad sack who lives with his mother,
Comes to pick up the meal cooked for him.
Smiling, *la fornaia* brings it out,
A capon fat as he is, trussed and steaming,
And casting over all an enchantment of rosemary,
Making every mouth a well of taste.
"Che profumo, eh!" says the baker, and she grins,
As he whose testimony we ignored
Takes his delectable supper from her hands
And steers it past our eyes into the night
To feast on by himself or with his mother,
While we, watching him go, wish we could have some.

Butterflies Under Persimmon

I heard a woman
      State once that because
He peered so closely

At a stream of ants
      On the damp, naked
Limb of a fruit tree,

She fell for her husband.
      She wanted to be studied
With that attention,

To fascinate as if
      She were another species,
Whose willingness to be

Looked at lovingly
      Was her defense, to be
Like a phenomenon

Among leaves, a body
      That would make him leave
His body in the act of loving,

Beautifully engrossed.
        I can't remember what
She looked like. I never met

The husband. But leaning close
        To the newly dropped
Persimmon in the wet grass,

And the huddle of four
        Or five hungry satyrs,
Drab at first glance, the dull

Brown of age spots, flitting
        Away in too many
Directions, too quickly

To count exactly, small
        As they are, in the shade
At the tree's base; leaning

Out of the sunlight, as if
        I could take part in the feast there,
Where, mid-September,

The persimmons drop,
　　　So ripe and taut a touch
Can break the skin;

Leaning close enough
　　　To trouble the eye-spotted
Satyrs, no bigger than

Eyelids, and the fritillaries,
　　　Their calmer companions,
Like floating shreds of fire,

Whose feet have organs
　　　Of taste that make their tongues
Uncoil in reflex with

Goodness underfoot,
　　　I thought of that woman's
Lover, there on my belly

In sun and shadow,
　　　And wished I could be like that.

Astragaloi

We know there must be consciousness in things,
    In bits of gravel pecked up by a hen
To grind inside her crop, and spider silk
    Just as it hardens stickily in air,
And even those things paralyzed in place,
    The wall brick, the hat peg, the steel beam
Inside the skyscraper, and lost, forgotten,
    And buried in ancient tombs, the toys and games.
Those starry jacks, those knucklebones of glass
    Meant for the dead to play with, toss and catch
Back of the hand and read the patterns of,
    Diversions to beguile the endless time,
Never to be picked up again.... They're thinking,
    Surely, all of them. They are lost in thought.

Old Acquaintance

White-throated sparrow, the century is beginning.
   The years ahead are waiting like white seeds.
      History is your silvery evening call,
         Whistling the name of another place you love
            As you return, then go back into hiding,
               The browns and brights of winter in your feathers.

Small migrator, we watch as you ignore
   History altogether, all that is not seeds,
      In synch with seasons but not any event
         That stops a human being with a thought
            (Though this event has stopped me). Your wings flex
               Like shadows of the icecap and the leaves.

You are as you have always been, we hope.
   If one of us moves too quickly, you depart.
      You travel in neat kin groups over latitudes.
         You prefer to eat the seeds spread on the ground.
            The centuries have changed, there are new numbers.
               We are counting on many things, including you.

Fox Night

What have I done to merit that regard?
Seeing the fox, I thought of diction like that:
Merit that regard, as if the wild demanded
A formal recognition of its grace
When passing through our world. What *had* I done,
So that I thought the world, at least my family,
Should know a fox was looking back at me?
V of head and ears tilted, lean waist
Humped with a serpent's frozen listening,
It poised like the green snake on the back road
My girls and I had found one summer day,
Back when we found such things on summer days.
The snake had let us study, then urge it on
To belly-waddle sideways, s- and elbowing,
Clumsy only because we made it hurry,
Into the roadside vetch and vinca blossoms.
It had endured us with the noble patience
Of relics, like an ancient copper bracelet
Uncoiled. And yet it flicked its tongue out, testing.
But with the fox, its red fur drenched in shadows,
Only the tail-tip gathering enough streetlight
To show its whipped-up, egg-white whiteness, I
Was by myself, come out to stow some trash,

The TV muttering in the den behind me.
The fox had come to eat the fall persimmons,
The harvest of the tree in our front yard,
Acknowledged me, and turned away, of course,
And crossed the road back through a screen of oaks,
A wall that halved the sky, with chinks of starlight.
There was no one to instruct, no one to show
That happiness, though speechless, could be shared.
And so I made a comment to myself
In language that, if I'd repeated it,
Might have made my daughters look at one another
And wonder at the nature of the world.

As Close as Breathing

Called or not called, God is present.
—Delphic Oracle

The flicker doesn't know his call's not needed,
But he's not calling God. He lifts his beak
To show his black bib, as the females chuckle
Off in the oaks somewhere. They hear him all right.
The metal gutters make a fine percussion.

If God is present, why then aren't we talking?

The sugar water feeder stews in the sunshine.
The mud daubers fall asleep there, suckling.
The hummingbirds blur past. Last summer
One came with a ruby wart on her neck,
An imperfection that was almost perfect.

Does God assume our silence is a call?

If I write down the day I see the first swift
(Never the same day but always April),
It's not a prayer, though it may count as one.
They like grade schools where one cold chimney stands,
An obelisk in a cloud of darting hieroglyphs.

Words too can be as close to us as breathing.

A spider's dragline, glinting like a thought,
Trolls through depths of shade and morning light.
The hemlock limbs bob as if at anchor.
And a pair of downy woodpeckers swoops up
To the seed bell at my study window. Everything answers.

Everything says back, "I am present, too."

Shyness of the Muse in an Almond Orchard

The gray-green husks are opening. The wasps
And spiders build up high.
The vulture steps in from the field adjacent
And waddles down the row, first to claim
The rabbit clipped by the mower.
Dust mates with heat and spins at the least movement.

It's lonely for him but he doesn't know it.
Crouched atop his tractor,
He wheels out of a corridor of trees,
Wobbling on huge, flat-sided clods, and turns
To re-enter, stripping gears,
Engaging the mower's blades against the silence.

The stand is deep enough to have a heart
With nothing human in it
But a heart, webbed and humming and afraid.
At twilight, when he grinds through on his engine,
Buck, doe, and fawn
Unfold their knees and disappear like birds.

And I, as yet unimportant, am unseen,
Unrecognized, unknown,
Under the drooping boughs he has to lift,
Slowing and downshifting, his T-shirt pocked
With snags, his smooth chest bleeding.
A branch recoils and whips across his back.

Away from that, from leaves and mantises
That prickle his arms and face,
Out in the open evening, he feels taller—
Twenty years old, determined to remember
Heat, dust, and sound,
But not that I was here, that he was lonely.

In the Tube

They beat the edge
  Of the dawn light,
    The pearly pre-glow

Right at their heels,
  The three boys
    Carrying the fourth

Rolled in a sheet.
  They all had taken
    Something the night

Before in a beach
  House and this one
    Drowned in his sleep.

They acted quickly,
  These instinctive
    Athletes who cross

The faces of tons
  Of crushing water
    Which refrain

From curling over
    And burying them
        Alive because they

Are nimble, quick,
    Tuned to the wit
        Of their survivors'

Bodies. They hurried
    From the running car
        And laid their friend

Like a Sunday paper
    On his parents' doorstep,
        And drove off to

The place where the sharp
    New light would score
        The wave crests and they

Would ride below them,
    Dodging the onrush.

In Church with Hart Crane

This white Doubleday Anchor book
With the fuchsia pink M of the Brooklyn Bridge on the cover
Was my prayerbook in a church without prayerbooks.
I sat in the back shadows, knowing God could see
And so could my father speaking in the pulpit.
And I read, "It was a kind and northern face"
And liked that one and liked "Repose of Rivers"
Even more, as the singing river lost itself,
Hearing "wind flaking sapphire," in the sea
"Beyond the dykes." There was a sea beyond
The holy space behind my father's back,
Beyond the baptistry that cupped its portion,
Unsalty, tepid, blessed to rinse off sin.
A block away the Pacific swarmed with its rivers
And the wind really did flake Sapphire,
And Emerald, and Ruby—names of streets.
And in my hands the white book hummed.
There was poetry equal to its voices
In the drab hymnal slotted in the pew
And in my father's sinuous braid of sentences.
But I wouldn't know that for years. He wanted me
To be good. I wanted to write a poem as good

As "Repose of Rivers," as "My Grandmother's
Love Letters," as "Black Tambourine," the three
I thought I understood.
                            How many awful times
I've sat in church since then, believing
That I was neither good nor good enough
To write the poems I thought I understood.
With Christ invisible on his bloodless cross,
With Crane dissolved in the spindrift a block away,
I read in church, and couldn't imagine either one
Seated beside me in his fishy clothes,
Putting a salty finger on the page, saying,
"Read this one again. You haven't gotten it."
The most important person in the room,
Among the visible, was robed and large
And knew what I was doing, reading poetry,
And didn't say a word. I would remember.
I *have* remembered, and in my classrooms ignore
The sleeping boys and girls and the waking dreamers
Turning toward the window like sunflowers,
While some delectable phantom, like Hart or Jesus,
Drifts past, beckoning.

The book still falls open to those poems,

The ones I bowed my head to as if in prayer,

Asking to be a river, a love letter, a black tambourine.

Dialect

I can't remember the air, the light, the voices
Of what I used to think of as my home.
I truly can't recall how people sounded.
So now, when I hear someone on the news,
That guileless Western accent tinged with Spanish
Or vice versa, musical and flat,
Makes me ask, "What *is* that?" Then, I know.
And natives here will ask me when I speak,
"Where you from?" I tell them Greater Los Angeles.
A seedy, little beachtown, I say proudly,
That now, I add, has been yuppified.
I say it was a middle class, working class town
Of Anglos, Mexicans, Asians, a Black family,
Draftsmen and riveters for McDonnell-Douglas,
Hughes Aircraft, Northrop, Garrett Air Research.
Sea fog watered the morning rush-hour traffic.
Kids snorkeled after school and drowned at parties.
A Nike missile base protected us.
Their finned white noses sniffed the onshore breeze
And one day they were trucked off into nowhere.
From their abandoned hill we could look deep
Into the graft on graft of inland cities
And watch the riot smoke, when it erupted,

Blend with the stinging gauze of urban haze.
My parents bought their house for 20 grand.
Today, somebody else's house, it's worth
Half a million dollars—a yellow stucco
Among blue, pink, and white ones, just like it.
The colors made the sameness all seem better.
And just to cut the idyll short, the boys
Of different colors I played football with
Could turn from running plays to drawing knives
And smash each other's windshields and exchange
Curses in each other's mother tongues.
The late-night surf-crash made us all sleep soundly.
I couldn't wait to leave. But thought I'd be back.
Today rain followed snow and hammered nailholes
In the breadlike whiteness covering the heart
Of the continent's heart. All the gutters are singing.
I can't remember the air, the light, the voices.
But that's a lie. I can. Together they
Answer the reporter's questions like experts,
Surveying burning blocks by helicopter.

Outside

God says to Adam and Eve, "This time nothing's forbidden.
You may have the garden and the fruit of every tree.
That tree's fruit will give you knowledge of good and evil.
The fruit of this tree, even better, will make you forget.
Eat all you want. Let bygones be bygones."
And so at once they go to find the wall
And the way out, eating as they go,
Burning as they go, going because just thinking
There is a wall makes them feel cramped. They cross
Rivers and mountains, seas, they find no wall.
They eat the fruit of knowledge and see the problem:
Without a wall, the world is all they have,
Crisscrossed by their progress, a vacant lot.
God reminds them, "Nothing is forbidden."
They eat the fruit of forgetfulness, and forget.

The Heavenly Ladder of John Klimax
12th-Century Byzantine Icon

Too many have gotten on the thick-runged sideways stair.
No wonder some must be pulled off and tugged down where
Hell swallows them headfirst. Hell-mouth is in a head
Like a boulder in the dirt, bald and well-fed.
The ladder almost reaches the windowledge on high
Where Jesus beckons, although he catches no one's eye.
And stuck up opposite like a decal of starry blue,
Angels with gilt haloes obscure each other's view.
So, why begin the climb toward heaven's sky of gold,
If on the way to the top, you lose your foothold?
The upward-staring throng under the fiery hill
Occupies stabler ground, albeit it's in hell.
Isn't aspiration enough to save a soul?
Is clumsiness the sin that puts you in the hole?
Or is it just dumb luck to be lassoed by an imp
Who makes the upset look as if you chose to jump?
In Byzantium the world was round as it ever was,
But doesn't look that way. And the eternal laws
Of God, like gravity, seem whimsically selective.
In Byzantium it was hard to get a true perspective.
But one thing is for sure: the ladder itself, though tall
Enough to besiege heaven, looks about to fall.

And the poor souls dropping off it, though helped in their
    descent
By spiteful, one-wing cherubs, may sense the imminent
Breakdown that is built into everything human,
From Byzantium to art, from ladders to heaven.

Canzone

There is a Renaissance painting of paradise
In which people, still in their human bodies,
Are embracing as if they'd just arrived in paradise
Or—because some are angels—were being welcomed to
    paradise.
Nobody in the picture looks like a ghost.
Even the angels, winged for paradise,
Wear embraceable bodies. It seems that paradise
For Giovanni di Paolo is a place of happy reunions.
And now, when we anticipate reunions
Like those in every moment, paradise
Is not exactly the place we hope to arrive.
It's been made complicated—that arrival.

Our destination is where we hope to arrive.
Simple enough but now a paradox,
Since now we cannot be certain of our arrival
And have to pray simply that we arrive.
And of course we hope to arrive in our human bodies,
The ones we've always known since our arrival
On earth, the ones for which there are no rivals
Imaginable, except as an Italian ghost
Has painted them. But who wants to be a ghost,

Even if it means being part of a revival,

Even in such a classic, reunited

As form and content, body and soul's reunion?

Let's face it, only the hardiest can see union

With art as a satisfying arrival.

For most of us, our daily lives unite

Our needs for love and work. And their smooth union

Is, come to think of it, a blissful paragon,

A reason to tell the partner of our union,

Talking about our day over dinner, united

In crunching through bread and salad, of our body's

Desire to be united with their body.

It's a good day that ends with such a union.

And though we might still love each other's ghost

And say so, what we desire is not a ghost.

What we desire is both the flesh and ghost,

The full consort together, the living union.

We know that's health. We know that this new ghost

Of rumor and apprehension is a ghost

Like the horizon line, always arriving.

And now we have to live with the kind of ghost

That gives a bad name to every ghost—
I mean to every airy sense of paradise
Where the good—which should mean all of us—find paradise,
Despite the blemishes we've stuck to our ghosts.
It all comes back, doesn't it, to the body?
We wish we'd never have to leave our bodies.

Or have to leave the way we think of our bodies.
Giovanni clothes the heavenly in the ghost
Of class and calling. He paints no naked bodies,
Despite our expectations of the body
In heaven, restored to a primeval union
With innocence and ignorance. He says we'll be those bodies
Identified as us, and so we'll dress our bodies
As we have understood them. Maybe after arriving
We'll come to understand that to arrive
In heaven is to embrace the hidden body.
After all, this is but an interpretation of paradise,
Which says we bring our world with us to paradise.

I'm glad Giovanni di Paolo saw the arrival
Of souls in paradise as a time for reunion,
And not merely a mingling of bodiless ghosts.

I wish I could believe in that promise of paradise
As deeply as I believe in this mortal body.

George Herbert

Who is wise enough today to be George Herbert,
    Who though he lost his temper could remain
Tractable to a loving, patient voice?
    Washing his parishioners' feet, as the collar chafed
And softened. Writing his fastidious verses,
    Like the coffin-shaped stones of his century,
Decked with skulls and propped in churchyard corners.
    Death, a puddle of dust, drew under his door,
Like talcum powder, clinging to his shoes.
    And love, whose board he hammered with his fist,
Drew him in and offered him its meat,
    That ambiguous unambiguous word. George Herbert
Was wise enough to sit and clean his plate.

Goya's *Saint Peter Repentant*

A little hilltop stepped on by a glacier—that's how he looks,
  his bald head nearly flat,
And the upward turning dog's eyes humble as heather, and
  the tufts of eyebrow and beard sheepish.
He's draped with orange clay and a curving seam of
  granite—his clothes.
I've never seen thicker hands in a painting of a saint. I've
  seen hands like them
On men who showed me how to do work that would wilt
  me by lunch hour, making me understand,
Later, why roofers spend half their lunch hour lying in
  shade, if there is any, one arm flung over their eyes.
He looks sorry. He already has the keys, and yet he's sorry.
  Asking forgiveness is hard work.

Compare El Greco's Peter doing the same thing. Everything
  lengthens heavenward.
Beautiful, yes, and saintly, yes, but not Peter. Of all the
  apostles—the earthiest, the most creaturely.
He said one thing that pleased Jesus, though it pleased him
  mightily, and others that disappointed them both.
In Goya's painting, the keys to heaven lie on a stone like a
  mattress corner, their loops lapped by a fold of Peter's robe,

As if Peter, not yet a saint, didn't see them, or had put them aside until he finished his work.

The Excitement

My grandfather was given to believing
In ghosts beside the Holy Ghost. As a boy
He felt an invisible hand clap on his head
As a voice murmured, "You are in my power."
As a man he heard his mother's voice in the pulpit.
In some lights he could picture people's souls
As shrouds of fog or stray bits of apparel,
Shirttails poking out, secret banners waving.
He knew what faith could do, that hidden star
Imploded at the galaxy's black heart,
And he had faith. He wanted a technique.
He knew there was a way to make his faith
Devour its cosmic doubts and spit them back
As the moving mountains of both space and time.
Time led him on to death. And space confined him.
He thought—if he could only pull them apart
And not unweave himself. He believed his soul
Was safe, because it also hid within him,
Separate and pristine, a bead of meaning,
A seed in time and space which, once beyond them,
Would blossom in eternity, just waiting.
But let him move this salt shaker across the table.
If he could do that, simply with a thought,

What couldn't he do? What my grandfather wanted
Was mind enough to move things with a thought.
And he believed that faith was a technique,
But there had to be others. Jesus came
To tell him there were no others, and faith itself
Was not invented to move salt shakers.

But Jesus came to him. Who wouldn't want that?
Who wouldn't want to walk with him in a garden,
On a sunny day, in a cloister of fresh flowers?
He would make you feel special and would not flatter,
But speak about the world that you could make,
You would have the power to make, which he would give you.
No one could get enough of such a person.
Charisma (the heroin of personality)—
My grandfather wanted to have that, too:
To be the one the young monks flocked behind,
Quacking their questions, and to stop every so often
To answer them like a cloud across the sun—
Not ominous but with refreshing coolness.
Gandhi, it is said, took walks like that.
One entered in the flow of his current interests,
In honeybees, or salt recovery, or spinning wheels.

Who wouldn't want in the cool of the day to walk
With one who knew everything about you,
More even than you knew? That was the secret.
The faith that walked on water was a power
My grandfather wanted, with its homely gifts
For treating time and space like salt and pepper.
A dash of either and the real was changed
Into the spicy soup of the unreal.
To taste that, and to make that simply happen.

And doesn't it matter to want something better
And not a raise or more job self-esteem,
But something on a plane so rarefied
You lived there like a migrant hummingbird
Or monarch butterfly, crossing the Gulf,
Going north or south and feeding on the sugar
Of ecstasy, existing in that wingbeat,
The sky, the expanse of water, no land in sight?
To put his hand through air into the future,
And heal the dying child. To reach back with ten fingers
And raise the loved one, waiting in the grave.
Because he knew that Christ had done these things,
My grandfather wanted to do them, too.

He wanted to leave his mark on the eternal,
To manipulate the supernatural stuff
That he was sure was everywhere, like the air waves.
And on the radio he threw his voice
Against the willing air that rippled with it.
He called himself the Shepherd of the Air
And gathered his flock of insubstantial strays
From the antennas of Los Angeles.

I've told you this so you can know this man,
My grandfather, a little, as I tell my story,
The only real ghost story I know,
A holy ghost story, complete with blood and terror,
For it unfolds at night, and someone or something
Risen from the dead plays a crucial role
At scaring the living Jesus out of somebody.
It may be Jesus himself who did the scaring.

It was a dry and cool November evening.
Los Angeles collected all its lights,
Some still, some strung on moving threads,
Into its basin beside the ocean's darkness.

This was the vastness where my grandfather worked,

Alone in his church office, recording a sermon

On tape, and playing it back, and hearing himself

Explain the spiritual power of some new thing,

Some drug or diet or mental exercise

That had excited him. The ghost was coming,

The first he'd ever seen, after years of wishing

That he could see them everywhere.

Hypnotist, Metaphysician, Parapsychologist,

Quester in the Dreamworld, Channeler,

These were roles he played or he pretended.

And now a real ghost, torn from the cosmos,

Was coming to his office to address him.

There was a step, ringing on the stairwell,

Although my grandfather couldn't hear it,

Or hear the doorknob turn, the presence enter,

For he was listening to himself quote scripture,

"Behold, I stand at the door and knock." Red letters

His voice turned into living words, like song.

Then, out of the tangled mesh of chapter and verse,

The blood of Jesus' speech on the filmy page

Spilled suddenly across the carpeted floor.

My grandfather looked up and saw the man,
And not as in his Bible recitations.
Bleeding, yes, but dressed in business clothes.
In fact, dressed as he was in business clothes,
About my grandfather's height, about his size,
Bald with a little silver hair combed sideways,
And wearing horn-rimmed glasses, lips parted
To speak. The ghost had on the same white shirt.
And both wore ties, the same tie, with the same knot.
But Grandfather couldn't see these things for the blood,
The blood coming from the hands and feet—
Bare feet in a business suit, with familiar hands,
And the blood from the famous wounds printing the carpet
And spreading over the things on the glass-topped desk.
The bleeding man in the dark suit looked familiar.
And his voice, too, sounded strange in the same way
Grandfather's voice did when he played it back.
But the question that he asked as he stood there bleeding
Was not one Grandfather ever asked himself:
"Why are you wasting your time on all this nonsense?"
He saw a soul wounded by his existence
And told the world and us it was Jesus Christ.

The years into old age and death were set then.
And I have often thought about those years.
For this was the peak moment in family history,
The Lord come unto Granddad to rebuke him
And all the supernatural confirmed.
For he did not turn away from his desires,
But took a new way, or an old way he'd forgotten.
Life with the Holy Spirit, as he called it,
Led him to crowds as he had never known them,
The leaning forward masses who could see
Something peculiar that they wanted, too,
Bathing the old man in its thrilling spotlight.
Even as his body gave up its powers—
Abandoning a right hand's cunning, breaking a hip,
And draining from the corner of his mouth—
Wheeled into the presence of believers,
He basked in their true love and stuck by his story.
They led him a merry dance until he died.

Lord Chemistry

"the kingdom of God is within you"
—Luke 17: 21

The kingdom is inside somewhere all right.
   It's tucked in by a fold of time and space,
So that the way that always feels like out
   Is in. All right. Where there had been a door,
Instead I rapped against a plinth of slate.

Where there had been a medium that carried
   My voice into the court or den or chamber
Of that one I appealed to, who had answered
   With the best answer self-love could invent,
There was a blank and no vocabulary.

I didn't like it. And I saw the dawn,
   And it was like the bleakness in the eyes
Of parents kept awake beside sick children
   Whose fevers have endured the night unbroken.
I was my child and begged for sleep like life.

And no one listened, because no one could.
   It was so simple what had stopped my voice:
An oracle prescribed for me, a wad

40

Of molecules whose message was, "Your God
Is simple as a change of mind or drug."

And so I changed the drug that changed my mind.
    You know those dreams of houses, where new rooms
Appear in dwellings that you thought you knew?
    Mine opened on a cloister where the sky
Admitted me into its lullaby.

Five Psalms

1.

Let us think of God as a lover
  Who never calls,
Whose pleasure in us is aroused
  In unrepeatable ways,
God as a body we cannot
  Separate from desire,
Saying to us, "Your love
  Is only physical."
Let us think of God as a bronze
  With green skin
Or a plane that draws the eye close
  To the texture of paint.
Let us think of God as life,
  A bacillus or virus,
As death, an igneous rock
  In a quartz garden.
Then, let us think of kissing
  God with the kisses
Of our mouths, of lying with God,
  As sea worms lie,
Snugly petrifying
  In their coral shirts.

Let us think of ourselves
　　As part of God,
Neither alive nor dead,
　　But like Alpha, Omega,
Glyphs and hieroglyphs,
　　Numbers, data.

2.

First forgive the silence
　　That answers prayer,
Then forgive the prayer
　　That stains the silence.

Excuse the absence
　　That feels like presence,
Then excuse the feeling
　　That insists on presence.

Pardon the delay
　　Of revelation,
Then ask pardon for revealing
　　Your impatience.

Forgive God
　　For being only a word,
Then ask God to forgive
　　The betrayal of language.

　　3.

God of the Syllable
　　God of the Word
God Who Speaks to Us
　　God Who Is Dumb

The One God　The Many
　　God the Unnameable
God of the Human Face
　　God of the Mask

God of the Gene Pool
　　Microbe　Mineral
God of the Sparrow's Fall
　　God of the Spark

God of the Act of God
　　Blameless　Jealous

God of Surprises
  And Startling Joy

God Who Is Absent
  God Who Is Present
God Who Finds Us
  In Our Hiding Places

God Whom We Thank
  Whom We Forget to Thank
Father God Mother
  Inhuman Infant

Cosmic Chthonic
  God of the Nucleus
Dead God Living God
  Alpha God Zed

God Whom We Name
  God Whom We Cannot Name
When We Open Our Mouths
  With the Name God Word God

4.

The new day cancels dread
  And dawn forgives all sins,
All the judgments of insomnia,
  As if they were only dreams.

The ugly confrontation
  After midnight, with the mirror,
Turns white around the edges
  And burns away like frost.

Daylight undoes gravity
  And lightness responds to the light.
The new day lifts all weight,
  Like stepping off into space.

Where is that room you woke to,
  By clock-light, at 3 A.M.?
Nightmare's many mansions,
  Falling, have taken it with them.

The new day, the day's newness,
  And the wretchedness that, you thought,

Would never, never depart,
   Meet—and there is goodbye.

A bad night lies ahead
   And a new day beyond that—
A simple sequence, but hard
   To remember in the right order.

   5.

Lord of dimensions and the dimensionless,
Wave and particle, all and none,

Who lets us measure the wounded atom,
Who lets us doubt all measurement,

When in this world we betray you
Let us be faithful in another.

Canticle

Beautiful repetition, the caress repeated, again,
That makes one say and repeat, "Don't stop."

Reiteration, restatement, the beat brushed into skin;
The pulse responding to breath, counted, touched.

Beautiful pattern of change, cyclical as blood,
The axle pivots, the planet wanders.

The moon comes back and leaves, a total story or slice
Of life, shining with meaning, like a life.

Beautiful repetition, the haze of new grass
Rises from scattered seeds, a green dawn.

A chickadee's claim rings the seed bell by the window.
The world tilts, too, a ball dented by song.

Look at it happen again, always in a new pattern:
Famine again, war, after the odd peace.

Habit, the great deadener, narrows our affections
To one face, reappearing in the mirror.

Look at it happen again, always for the first time:
Death of the father, the mother, absolute.

No way to bring them back, except to become them.
Tragic reenactment, beautiful repetition.

Song of Roland

Roland was a Paladin of Charlemagne,
And he was my mother's cousin. The Paladin
Served Charlemagne and died, blowing his horn.
The cousin spent a day with her at the fair
Over sixty years ago. The great Paladin
Enjoys an epic named after him.
The cousin is remembered as a big kid
Who never grew up. His first wife left him,
Taking only the pillows from the pool furniture.
Roland the epic hero was betrayed
By a fellow Paladin. Roland the cousin bought
A box of face powder for his younger cousin,
And on the octopus, which they had ridden
So often the owner let them ride for free,
He convinced her to open up the box.
Roland's horn resounds through ages
Of high school lit classes. There's a cloud
The carnie thinks is an explosion and stops
His ride, and banishes the powdered laughing children,
Roland, the young hero, and my mother
Creamy with dust in a new blue coat.
Roland's song comes down from the Pyrenees.
His namesake went back to school, after his wife left,

Became a mining engineer, worked in North Dakota,

Married again, learned after the death of his parents

He'd been adopted, was devastated, and died

In his late 30's of congenital heart failure. He lives on, though.

An old woman remembers that day at the fair

And as much of his life and fate as any of us

Is likely to have immortalized in song.

Over the River and Through the Woods

Back streets, byways, eroded, gouged, patched wide spots
Between chain link and cinder block,
Lanes too pretty a word, alleys too much glamour,
Channels of gravel, asphalt scar tissue, mud and gray dust,
Passages past doors without handles and empty parking lots
Where the leanest wine-dark vagrant
Hikes his pants up over his non-hips after pissing,
Or less than that, regions where no one does anything
Except pass through, shortcuts to lead garbage trucks to
    dumpsters,
Delivery trucks to loading docks, drunks to a place to sleep,
Charmless, rough, pitted and potholed,
Leafless, except for overlapping leaves of tar,
The last to be served and absolutely necessary,
Where milky coffee puddles turn to cracked frosting
And a wasp or butterfly (a cabbage white) wets its tongue,
Part of the radiant, hidden world, part of what makes it
Radiant, hidden, the world,
Places to baptize a sudden yen for new life,
On the way to grandmother's house.

The Reckless Father

A father can dissolve among the trees
That throng his neighborhood or dig a hole
And take the world down with him for a spell
Of brooding. He can get down on his knees.

Or, as her father did when he was low,
Put wife and children in the family car
And press the accelerator to the floor.
Outside of town, with no place to go,

He pushed the speedometer until the needle
Stopped at a hundred and ten or a hundred and twenty.
They passed the slower cars into the country
And faced the others coming and watched their nerve fail.

Fenders scraped and ripped. Cars ricocheted
And howled behind them off the road, red-shifting
Into the muted distance as, clear-sailing,
They breezed along on their wild way.

Or they would veer and bite dirt in a ditch
Up to the hubcaps, or overturn and spin

Into a lumpy field. And grateful in
The aftermath, say, "I'm alive" to their mother's touch.

His daughter grew up to tell this story laughing,
As listeners gasped, and trying to explain
That while her father was a dangerous man,
Surely it was better to keep him driving.

On Learning of a Child's Memory

Here is a milky web,
  A wheel of silk,
    Set back inside the hedge.
      And here is where

The honeysuckle spirals
  Up the light pole,
    And our pet cat,
      Chased round and round the garden

By a black lab who
  Wanted to be friends,
    Died and is buried.
      Here is the rose of Sharon

And the split stalk
  The termites came to live in.
    Here are the side-by-side
      Hedge-apple trees

That love each other
  And make flowers and fruit.

And here is the tour
   Of our old backyard.

Your hand in mine,
   You repeat what I describe.
    There is a spider
     Wrapping up a bee.

There is the place
   We buried Lyda Rose.
    You're four years old.
     Beyond the hedge

Are dragons, hurtling
   Shadows, blown down trees,
    The sprawling years,
     Too much to name, too much.

Here is the squirrels'
   Unburied treasure,
    The heap of ripe hedge-apples
     We piled up for them.

The richest shade is here,
  The coolest air,
    Under the trees
      Outside my study window.

And unknown to me
  Your memory will be
    Not of our walks here
      In another time,

But of the windowsill
  Where my face shadows
    A page, glowering,
      Following a pen,

And you outside, below,
  Hidden breathlessly.

The Wind

Worrying about the children I kept waiting
   To be relieved and walked to the Gallery
On a frigid morning in the nation's capital.
   Great clouds of vapor smoking from the street-vents
Unraveled the long stone views of public buildings.
   And small among them, private and insistent,
My fretting was a nightmare nakedness,
   Which must be obvious but no one sees.
I'd come to town on business. It was finished.
   I had a little time and stalked through rooms
Of likenesses and paint that still looked wet
   On the old masters and the younger masters.
I looked around, wanting to be changed,
   And passed the pictures as if they were stalled traffic
And I had chosen to get out and walk.
   Then faced the modest painting by Vallotton,
The Wind, in the East Wing, and walked on,
   And then returned and stood before it, feeling
A southern breeze begin, hearing a hymn,
   "Breathe on me, breath of God." Eight trees were bending
From right to left across the picture plane.
   So wind-altered I couldn't give them names,

They bowed away yet faced what made them bow.
   The undergrowth beneath them caught the sunlight
And handled it with fronds of yellow shining.
   We were looking up from the floor of Paradise—
I saw that suddenly—and God was calling,
   Warming the cool of the day with his vast breath.
The trees, his angels, pointed where he was looking.
   It wasn't clear if we had fallen yet.
But if we had, this green half-kneeling stir,
   In which things rooted and inevitable were swaying,
Might soothe his wrath and make him think again.
   The sympathetic magic of the paint
Was like a prayer sent both from the past,
   A gift from the dead artist, and from the future,
Vaulting the barrier of all that had been done
   And fixed forever, bathing the judged world
In a wish to soften harshness, everything leaning.
   This wind, painted by Félix Vallotton,
In 1910, somewhere in France, conveyed
   Counsel like a draft of medicine.
And in that counsel, drawn over my anger,
   So that it passed through every leaf of it,

(For anger is what I felt, a cloudy ire

  At children who were ceasing to be children)
Came what I had to do. The picture said,

  "Forgive them. And let them live their lives."

The Secret Ocean

When you were little girls, I brought you here
    To light weaving on water among trees,
With one of you beside me, walking along,

    The other on my shoulders, talking to herself.
We found this place beside a baseball field
    In a flood plain, flooded with meadowlarks.

And on a jut of fossil-bearing limestone
    We pitched our half-hour camp. Strewn on rock
Were shells that had been eaten out that morning,

    Pearly debris of crayfish, turbinate snails.
The torrent raveled past, a golden craftwork,
    No deeper than reflection. A speckled dancing

Took place upon the wavelets and the air,
    A water strider sort of dance, a shifting
Greened by the leaves like lenses overhead.

    I think I named it after one of you,
Claire's Secret Ocean, Zoë's Secret Sea,
    Far from the actual oceans you'd not seen yet.

61

Under the cottonwoods, among acacia stalks,
　　We watched the nimble acts of light and shadow,
The harmless tumult, the dimpled water tension.

　　Neither of you knew that we were there
To calm and change the color of my thought,
　　To ease its glaring pressure for a moment.

And we have been together other places
　　For the same reason, which I can now reveal—
There have been times I thought my head would crack,

　　Only to have you both demand ice cream.
It's been a long time since we've walked together
　　For reasons you didn't have to understand.

If you were younger I wouldn't be less fearful,
　　Now that the monster shadowing you is not
The wounded ego of your harmless father,

　　But something that would harm you if it could
And in old fashioned terms has had its way
　　With all of us. I think of the first, stunned day

Outside of Eden, going through the motions—
   No—learning motions no one had yet dreamed of.
And menace, like a new electric nimbus,

   Surrounding everything, invisibly.
And no one to walk with us but each other.
   And yet it could be that these private walks

To places like the secret ocean, trailing
   Beside a darkened, mute, distracted parent,
Were preparations for new valleys of the shadow,

   Fearing no evil, because someone was with you.

Summer

At the end of a bad year, the swifts
Offer their bodies to the air we breathe,
Saying, "This is the real world," as she did,
Turning to me on the bed. "This is
The real world."

               And on the eve of another
Uncertainty, the fireflies cover their lamps.
Their blazing codes, sinking with us
To sleep, echo, "This is the real world. This
Is the real world."

               And as the dogwoods
Forfeit their beauty, and August ignites
Its first leaf, there is consolation
In knowing that this is the real
World.

          For she was naked. And I believed her.

Kuan Yin

The blanc de chine porcelain many-armed goddess offers us
Something held loosely in each of her many hands.
It may be a key or an axe, a tongue or a flower,
But whatever it is, it is ours for the taking. That's clear.
She herself, so the story goes, gave up arms and eyes
To save the life of her father who hated her goodness.
And when he was saved he asked the name of the donor
(It was 7th-century China, but *donor*'s the right word)
And learned from his doctors that his daughter had saved
    his life.
She had given her arms and eyes, and they ground them up
Into a paste which they fed to her ill, estranged father.
(How many fairy tales can you remember, fables and myths,
Involving the irony of eating your own flesh and blood?)
Restored he went to her, but it was too late for forgiveness.
And instead of an armless, eyeless stalk of pity,
He found the new goddess, a dazzling wheel in the air,
Her radiant spokes the thousand arms of compassion
And her eyes multiplied, too, like the eyes of heaven.
As she faced him for the last time, she was like a mandala
Where he glimpsed the inch of his life, her gift to him,
Just as she left him, just as she disappeared.
And now, here in a glass museum box,

Aesthetically lit to show she's a work of art,
She lives in her glazed gestures beyond her sacrifice,
Beyond hatred, suffering, and goodness, beyond her story,
Although it's the story that makes us understand.

Coyotes

Is this world truly fallen? They say no.
For there's the new moon, there's the Milky Way,
There's the rattler with a wren's egg in its mouth,
And there's the panting rabbit they will eat.
They sing their wild hymn on the dark slope,
Reading the stars like notes of hilarious music.
Is this a fallen world? How could it be?

And yet you're crying over the stars again
And over the uncertainty of death,
Which you suspect will divide us all forever.
I'm tired of those who broadcast their certainties,
Constantly on their cellphones to their redeemer.
Is this a fallen world? For them it is.
But there's that starlit burst of animal laughter.

The day has sent its fires scattering.
The night has risen from its burning bed.
Your tears are proof that love is meant for life
And for the living. And this chorus of praise,
Which the pet dogs of the neighborhood are answering
Nostalgically, invites our answer, too.
Is this a fallen world? How could it be?

A Pair of Tanagers

The scarlet male, his green mate, their black wings
Beside the AC unit in the dull dirt:

They look at first like a child's abandoned toys.
But ants and iridescent flies have found them,

Working along the seams of the shut beaks
And the dark indentations of the eyelids.

You want to give something like this a moral:
Like, the woods these days are full of hard illusions,

Or, never fly north if you think you're flying south,
Or, stay above rooftops; if you meet yourself

Coming, it's too late; death is a big surprise.
And their death together certainly startles us.

Stopped short. But how recently in the rain forest,
How recently in the place they were first named,

Reflected on the Amazon, the Orinoco,
Headlong from Brazil, into our window.

You want to give something like this a moral
Or see it as an omen, as a portent.

And then, the long journeying comes to mind,
Together such a distance, to this end.

Visitors

They move about the bedside at the end,
Detach from mist and clothe themselves in light,
Or so I've heard. As Grace was dying, there came
A nurse who pulled a sheet over her chest.
Another was a little death from childhood
Who lay his head beside her on the pillow.
The murmur that I heard was "preparation."
They were preparing her for her own visit.

—

Charles Wesley asked, "Visit us with Thy salvation."
Don't be a stranger. Visit. Come and see us.

—

My visitors walk down a corridor. No,
They take their seats. No, they pull the curtain.
My visitors invade and go house to house.
They see the curtain move, they come to the door.

—

We're all visitors here. We have all come to see.
"Go see life, go see the Planet Earth,"
Says something I'll call the Mighty Invitation.

———

I visited her, and she looked like a million dollars.
She said, "Do you just want to see what I look like?
What took you so long to call?" She stood among pictures
And prices, explained the values
To small investors. I suppose she owned the Kandinsky,
A small early one, a matron with a parasol,
Drowned in blue light. She was happy to see me. I was
Happy to see her. We had a nice visit.

———

Cross-armed, forehead placed on the glass,
Counting over again the sparse Sunday turnout,
My father watches the sprinklers toil, frail lilies of brilliance,
Soaking the yellow patch of sandy lawn.
The gulls, like diacritical marks on the sky-blue sentence,
Pass over but do not visit. They are not visitors.

—

We can't relive the past. But we can visit.

—

Angels are messengers, but when they visit,
They have not come to see us or how we are.
They speak, looking through us. They see what we will
    become
When we have understood why they have come.

—

Or else they do not see us at all. They appear
At their austere destinations, packets of gilded speech,
Unwrapped and signed for. And their duties done.

—

The astronomer said, "I like the idea of life
Falling to earth, rather than rising from it,
Riding the vector of rain, condensed

From a comet's tail, sweeping through the atmosphere."
And when he spoke, these visitors circulating
Through decades, centuries, millennia,
Began to turn in the light of his mind,
An icy crown, lit jewel by jewel,
Or Goya's hat of candles for his night work,
Reported by an unexpected visitor.

—

Births are visitations, first and last. Tongues
Of fire visit the tops of the welcoming world.
But then, the new arrivals stay.
We watch our children's sojourns
Extend past any sense of being visits.
Who grants the visas for these foreigners?
And then, who says their time is up?
Off they are sent, into their lives
As if into new countries where we,
If we follow, will always be visitors.

Prayer for Our Daughters

May they never be lonely at parties
Or wait for mail from people they haven't written
Or still in middle age ask God for favors
Or forbid their children things they were never forbidden.

May hatred be like a habit they never developed
And can't see the point of, like gambling or heavy drinking.
If they forget themselves, may it be in music
Or the kind of prayer that makes a garden of thinking.

May they enter the coming century
Like swans under a bridge into enchantment
And take with them enough of this century
To assure their grandchildren it really happened.

May they find a place to love, without nostalgia
For some place else that they can never go back to.
And may they find themselves, as we have found them,
Complete at each stage of their lives, each part they add to.

May they be themselves, long after we've stopped watching.
May they return from every kind of suffering

(Except the last, which doesn't bear repeating)
And be themselves again, both blessed and blessing.

Peyton Hoge

THE AUTHOR

Mark Jarman was born in Mount Sterling, Kentucky, and grew up in California and Scotland. He is a professor of English at Vanderbilt University in Nashville, Tennessee. He is the author of seven books of poetry: *North Sea* (1978), *The Rote Walker* (1981), *Far and Away* (1985), *The Black Riviera* (1990), *Iris* (1992), *Questions for Ecclesiastes* (1997), and *Unholy Sonnets* (2000). Jarman's awards include a Joseph Henry Jackson Award for his poetry in 1974, three NEA grants in poetry in 1977, 1983, and 1992, and a fellowship in poetry from the John Simon Guggenheim Memorial Foundation for 1991–1992. His book *The Black Riviera* won the 1991 Poets' Prize. *Questions for Ecclesiastes* was a finalist for the 1997 National Book Critics Circle Award in poetry and won the 1998 Lenore Marshall Poetry Prize from the Academy of American Poets and *The Nation* magazine. His poetry and essays have been published widely in such periodicals and journals as *The American Poetry Review, The Gettysburg Review, The Hudson Review, The New Yorker, Poetry, The Yale Review,* and *The Southern Review*. During the 1980s he and Robert McDowell founded, edited, and published the controversial magazine *The Reaper*. Jarman makes his home in Nashville, Tennessee with his wife, the soprano Amy Jarman, and their daughters, Claire and Zoë.